Hidden in Plain Sight: Animal Camouflage

Elsie Belback

Rourke
Educational Media

rourkeeducationalmedia.com

Teaching Focus:
Vocabulary: Adjectives- Adjectives are words that describe. Look in the book. Find the words that describe (For example: giant, big, quick, deep).

Before Reading:

Building Academic Vocabulary and Background Knowledge
Before reading a book, it is important to set the stage for your child or student by using pre-reading strategies. This will help them develop their vocabulary, increase their reading comprehension, and make connections across the curriculum.
1. *Read the title and look at the cover. Let's make predictions about what this book will be about.*
2. *Take a picture walk by talking about the pictures/photographs in the book. Implant the vocabulary as you take the picture walk. Be sure to talk about the text features such as headings, Table of Contents, glossary, bolded words, captions, charts/ diagrams, or Index.*
3. Have students read the first page of text with you then have students read the remaining text.
4. *Strategy Talk – use to assist students while reading.*
   - Get your mouth ready
   - Look at the picture
   - Think…does it make sense
   - Think…does it look right
   - Think…does it sound right
   - Chunk it – by looking for a part you know
5. *Read it again.*
6. *After reading the book complete the activities below.*

Content Area Vocabulary
Use glossary words in a sentence.

coral
nooks
predators
prey
terrain
texture

After Reading:

Comprehension and Extension Activity
After reading the book, work on the following questions with your child or students in order to check their level of reading comprehension and content mastery.
1. *What does camouflage mean? (Summarize)*
2. *How does the chinstrap penguin camouflage itself? (Summarize)*
3. *Why would animals need the ability to blend in with their surroundings? (Summarize)*
4. *Can humans camouflage themselves? Explain. (Text to self connection)*

Extension Activity
Blending in with the environment is key for animal survival. You may have walked by animals and not known they were there! Now let's see if you can find objects that are hidden in plain sight. First you will need a box of multi-colored toothpicks or something similar. Separate them by color and record how many there are of each color. Then mix all the pieces together again. Take the pieces to a large grassy area like a field, playground, or lawn. Now, taking all the pieces in your hand, throw them in the air. Quickly pick up as many pieces as you can in one minute. Record how many of each color you found. Which colors were the easiest to find? The hardest? Why?

Close your eyes and start to count.
Now you see me. Now you don't!

Natural Camouflage

Animals do not always want to be seen. They need to hide from **predators**. They need to sneak up on **prey**.

Leopard

Moth

Some animals can hide in plain sight. They blend right in with their surroundings. The animals' color, **texture**, and patterns help them stay hidden.

Leaf-Tailed Gecko

Look closely. That tree has eyes! The leaf-tailed gecko almost disappears against the tree branch.

The gecko blends in with the tree bark. It hides in plain sight.

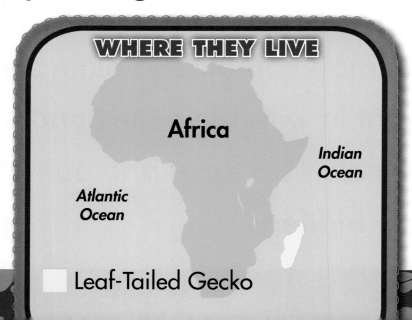

WHERE THEY LIVE

Atlantic Ocean

Africa

Indian Ocean

Leaf-Tailed Gecko

Leaf-Tailed Gecko

Thorny Devil

The thorny devil's bumps and spikes also allow it to collect water on any part of its body.

The thorny devil crawls across the desert floor. Its brown skin can change color. Its spikes look like rocks. Its color matches the ground.

The thorny devil blends in with the rocky ground. It hides in plain sight.

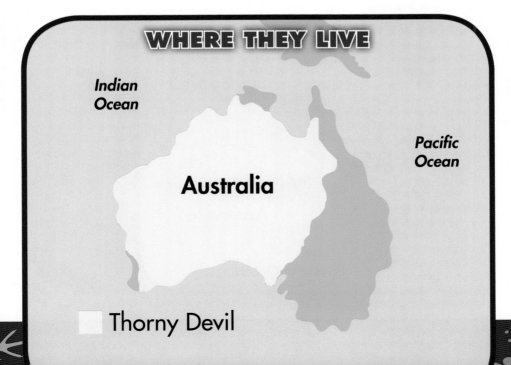

WHERE THEY LIVE

Indian Ocean

Pacific Ocean

Australia

Thorny Devil

Chinstrap Penguin

On land, the chinstrap penguin looks like snow and rock. When it swims, its belly looks like the bright sky. Its back looks like the dark sea.

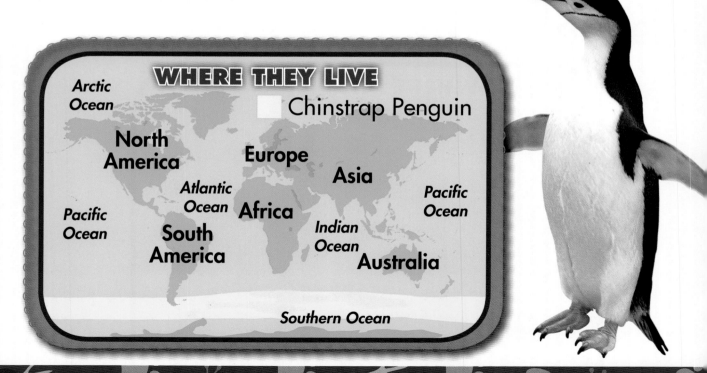

WHERE THEY LIVE

☐ Chinstrap Penguin

Arctic Ocean

North America

Europe

Asia

Atlantic Ocean

Africa

Pacific Ocean

Pacific Ocean

South America

Indian Ocean

Australia

Southern Ocean

The penguin blends in with the icy **terrain**. It hides in plain sight.

Chinstrap Penguins

Eastern Screech Owl

Whooo! Whooo! Who is in that tree? The Eastern screech owl hides in **nooks** and crannies. Its brown and white feathers match the tree.

The owl blends in with the forest tree trunks. It hides in plain sight.

Eastern Screech Owl

WHERE THEY LIVE

North America

Pacific
Ocean

Atlantic
Ocean

Eastern Screech Owl

Sidewinding Adder

It slithers and slides. The sidewinding adder moves like windblown sand. Its scales match the ground.

Sidewinding Adder

The adder blends in with the sandy ground. It hides in plain sight.

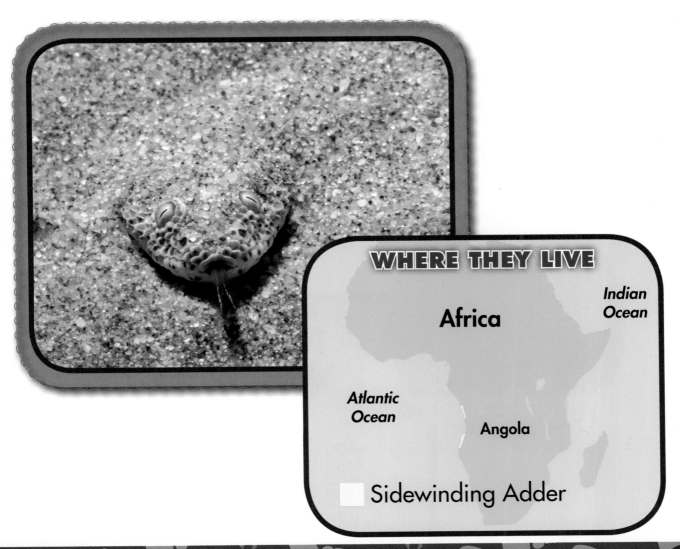

WHERE THEY LIVE

Africa

Indian Ocean

Atlantic Ocean

Angola

Sidewinding Adder

Pygmy Seahorse

The twisty, bumpy **coral** is the perfect place for a pygmy seahorse to hide. Its curly body looks just like the coral. It is well-hidden from hungry fish.

Pygmy Seahorse

WHERE THEY LIVE

Pacific Ocean

Indian Ocean

Australia

Pygmy Seahorse

The pygmy seahorse blends in with the prickly coral reef. It hides in plain sight.

Because they blend in so well with the coral, many pygmy seahorse species have only been discovered in the past 10 years.

Smooth Green Snake

The smooth green snake darts through the grass. It is almost unseen. The snake escapes from hungry birds.

Smooth Green Snake

The snake blends in with the green grass. It hides in plain sight.

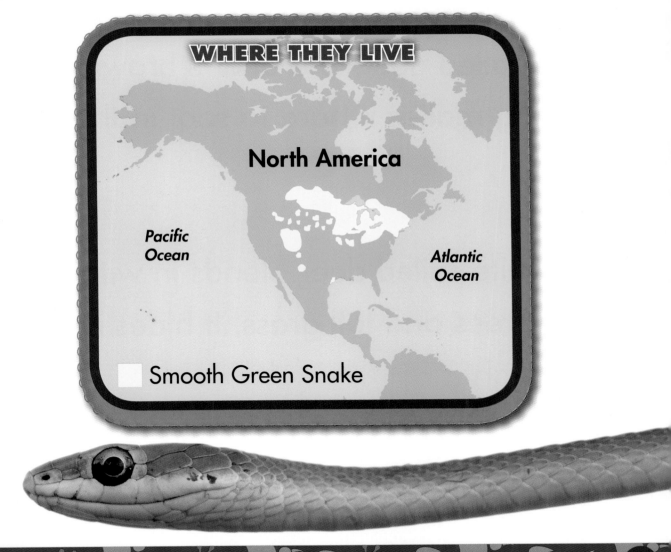

WHERE THEY LIVE

North America

Pacific
Ocean

Atlantic
Ocean

Smooth Green Snake

White-Tailed Deer

Oh deer! Hunters and predators stalk white-tailed deer. The deer's brown coloring makes it hard to spot in the forest.

The white-tailed deer blends in with the forest trees and tall grass. It hides in plain sight.

When animals are camouflaged, they have a great advantage of being hidden in plain sight.

WHERE THEY LIVE

North America

Atlantic Ocean

Pacific Ocean

South America

White-Tailed Deer

White-Tailed Deer

Photo Glossary

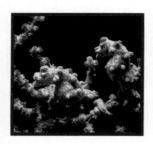 **coral** (KOR-uhl): Coral are animals that grow in an underwater environment.

 **nooks** (nuks): Nooks are small, private areas where animals hide.

 **predators** (PRED-uh-turz): Predators are animals that hunt other animals as food.

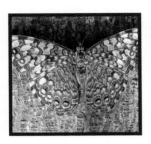

prey (pray): Prey is an animal that is hunted by other animals for food.

terrain (tuh-RAYN): Terrain is the physical features of a piece of land.

texture (TEKS-chur): Texture is the feel of something.

Index

About the Author

Elsie Belback lives and writes in Brooklyn, New York. She is an educator, children's book writer, and lifelong learner. Elsie has often spotted white-tailed deer grazing on the side of the New Jersey Parkway.

Meet The Author!
www.meetREMauthors.com

Websites

kids.nationalgeographic.com/kids/photos/gallery/animal-camouflage

dsc.discovery.com/tv-shows/curiosity/topics/animal-camouflage-pictures.htm

oakdome.com/k5/lesson-plans/powerpoint/animal-camouflage-pictures-and-information.php

www.rourkeeducationalmedia.com

PHOTO CREDITS: Cover: ©Gary Tognoni; title page: ©Mark Carroll; page 3: ©Mike Wilson Images Limited; page 4, 22: ©EcoPrint; page 5, 23: ©Wilm Ihlenfeld; page 7: ©Ryan M. Bolton; page 8, 23: ©Janelle Lugge; page 10: ©Leksele; page 11, 23: ©cunfek; page 13: ©artcphotos; page 14: ©Arno Dietz; page 15: ©Chantelle Bosch; page 16: ©timsimages; page 17, 22: ©Jung Hsuan; page 18: ©deepspacedave; page 19: ©Phillip W. Kirland; page 21: ©kalime; page 22 (middle): ©Alan Gleichman

Edited by: Jill Sherman
Cover design by: Jen Thomas
Interior design by: Rhea Magaro

Library of Congress PCN Data

Hidden in Plain Sight: Animal Camouflage/ Elsie Belback
(Close Up on Amazing Animals)
ISBN (hard cover)(alk. paper) 978-1-62717-635-4
ISBN (soft cover) 978-1-62717-757-3
ISBN (e-Book) 978-1-62717-878-5
Library of Congress Control Number: 2014934203
Printed in the United States of America, North Mankato, Minnesota

Also Available as:

ROURKE'S
e-Books